MW00901079

IN DUE SEASON

"And let us not grow weary of doing good,

for in due season, we will reap,

if we do not give up"

(Galatians 6:9).

Grace Neils Woodbridge

ISBN 978-1-0980-6703-8 (paperback)
ISBN 978-1-0980-6704-5 (digital)

Copyright © 2020 by Grace Neils Woodbridge

All rights reserved. No part of this publication may be reproduced, distributed, or transmitted in any form or by any means, including photocopying, recording, or other electronic or mechanical methods without the prior written permission of the publisher. For permission requests, solicit the publisher via the address below.

Christian Faith Publishing, Inc.
832 Park Avenue
Meadville, PA 16335
www.christianfaithpublishing.com

Unless otherwise indicated, all Scripture quotations are from the King James Version (KJV).

Other versions used
NIV—New International Version
NLT—New Living Translation

Cover photo by Roger Francis Clarke

Printed in the United States of America

CONTENTS

ACKNOWLEDGMENTS

Holy Spirit,

I give thanks and honor to God, the Holy Spirit, for His inspiration to write this book. It began with many questions that I had asked Him about and how His answers helped me through my life's difficulties.

Ruth Smith,

I would like to express my appreciation for your helping hands in getting this book out into the readers' hands. Thank you for your support and for your prayers.

DUE SEASON
WHEN IS IT DUE SEASON?

When you believe God says yes to whatever you asked Him for, you need to allow time for it to happen. There are some things that happen quickly, but some have their own appointed time. There is a time for everything and a season for every activity under the heavens (Ecclesiastes 3:1). Even when you have a "yes," you still want it right away, to have and enjoy as soon as possible. But God has His own timing and having faith in His timing makes it easier to wait.

There is a time between "yes" and "here it is!"

You don't start looking for "here it is" before you apply your faith to receive it, unless it's a miracle. Everything you receive from God comes by the way of faith. God says faith pleases Him; without faith it is impossible to please Him or believe in Him, and it is also impossible to receive a yes from Him without faith. Hebrews 11:6 says, "But without faith it is impossible to please Him; for he who would approach Him must believe that He is, and to the ones seeking Him He becomes the rewarder." When God gives you a vision, there is still a time of waiting before it becomes manifest. Habakkuk 2:3 says, "For the vision is yet for an appointed time; but at the end it will speak, and it will not lie. Though it tarries, wait *patiently* for it, because it will surely come."

You receive it supernaturally in your spirit, in the unseen realm, even though it is not yet manifest in the natural. You give birth to the *yes*, not God. He gives you the measure of faith to please Him, and you bring forth whatever you asked Him for. In Romans 12:3, it says, "For I say, through the grace of God given unto me, to every man that is among you, not to think of himself more highly than he ought to think, but to think soberly, as God has apportioned to each a measure of faith."

I was divorced and I wanted to marry again. I immersed myself in the word of God, the teaching and preaching of the Word. I searched the Scriptures to see what the mind of God said concerning marriage, and I saw in Genesis 2:18, "Then the Lord God said, 'It is not good for the man to be alone; I will make a helper who is just right for him.'" I continued to search, and Isaiah 34:16 says, "Search the book of the Lord and see what He will do: Not one of these birds and animals will be missing, and none will lack a mate, for the Lord has promised this. His Spirit will make it all come true." I saw where God provided mates for the birds and animals, and I believed He would also provide for me. I had confidence that God heard me, and it was His will for me to marry again. In 1 John 5:14–15, it says, "And this is the confidence that we have in Him, that if we ask anything according to His will, He hears us. And if we know that He hears us, whatever we ask, we know that we have the requests which we have asked from Him."

It was God's will! I waited and waited, and after several years, I asked God when was it time for due season? I asked God how I would know the appointed time or when my season had come? And one day while walking, this is what I believe I heard God say, "When you stand in faith and you believe you're to continue standing because it's not due season, as you continue standing you may get tired. But don't stop, it's not yet due season." *And when you feel you cannot continue standing, it's not due season;* it's not even near.

Hebrew 11:1 says, "Now faith is confidence in what we hope for and, assurance about what we do not see."

When you get to the place where you're standing in faith and speaking your faith, and it feels like there is nothing left in you to continue standing, it's still not due season. Due season comes when you are holding on to what you believe God for, and nothing can persuade you otherwise. Giants cannot persuade you; negative circumstances cannot move you. You are at the point where you will say, "I know God says yes, and I want it enough that if I get or don't get what I am standing for, I will continue to trust and serve God. I surrender my desires and my wants to you, God. At this point, if I get it, I will be happy, and if I do not get it, I will be content. Due season has come."

Due season came when I met my husband a couple years after I made that decision, and had surrendered to God. The seasons all come at their appointed time without delay, and the same is with you. Whatever you have asked God for, still He must be the center and the priority of what you want. You must surrender to Him your all. When pressure comes, open your mouth and remind God what He has promised and speak the word of God. Jeremiah 32:27 states, "Behold, I am the Lord, the God of all flesh, is there anything too hard for me?" If your desires are more important than wanting God, He will work with you until He becomes your priority. You must want God more than your desires.

And having done all, stand; and when you have done everything you know to do, stand. Stand, and receive the manifestation of your heart's desires through your faith and His will.

For example. You interview for a promotion at your work. Your resume is excellent. You meet all the requirements for the position. You believe that you will be successful; everything is going in your favor. You can just taste it; you see it happening, and you see yourself sitting at a desk in the office, and you say to yourself, "I've got this. It's a done deal."

They know your work history. You are always punctual, the first to start work and the last to leave. You tell all your friends that you will be working in a new position, and you calculate the salary increase that you would be making. You plan to get a new car, the one you have is old and worn out, and you are also looking forward to buying a home.

Your faith affirmation is strong; there is no way anything can go wrong. You have the confidence and assurance that you're going to get the job because you have a strong faith, and you have done all that you know to do. You're excited, and you're standing.

A few weeks later the manager calls you into his office, and you are smiling. He asks you to have a seat and you sit down across from him. He makes some relaxed small talk, then after a few minutes, he says, "I have some good news for you and some bad news."

You are so sure that the new position is yours! You did not hear the words *bad news*!

The manager starts talking about the new changes that the company will be making, then he says, "We have interviewed several applicants. You're a good worker, and we are happy to have you working for the company [they are happy, but you're not], and although you have an excellent resume, we have decided to offer the position to another applicant. He has graduated in the expertise and the skills we are looking for in the position."

Immediately you are overwhelmed with fear and sadness. You cannot believe what you heard. In your heart, you already own the position (and even though you felt like you owned the position, it might not be yours, for that which is yours cannot be taken from you). You begin to talk to yourself about how positive you were and how you were standing strong in faith and how sure you were that the job was yours.

You go home after work; you are depressed and angry. When the phone rings, you don't pick it up. For the rest of the evening, you shut yourself away from friends, and you stay all alone by yourself. The next day you go to work, but you are not communicating with anyone.

You avoid your coworkers and continue to remain angry. Prior to this, the energy around you was positive, but after the interview, the energy around you is toxic and you are thinking, *Why did this happen? Why didn't I get the job?* Your anger begins to turn toward God; you did everything that you had learned in faith to do. You memorized the scripture and meditated on it saying, "Now this is the confidence that we have in Him, that if we ask anything according to His will, He hears us. And if we know that He hears us, whatever we ask, we know that we have the petitions that we have asked of Him" (1 John 5:14–15).

What went wrong? You ask yourself. You did all the right things in your expectancy for the position, but you put your trust in the company's manager and not your heavenly Father. You did everything right, but your trust was in the wrong place. Trust is to believe, and you believed in the company you worked for instead of God, so when the new position fell through, you fell with it; you couldn't stand! You did not build your faith on the rock, Christ Jesus, but you built your faith on the sinking sand (the manager), and you could not stand.

When you heard the position was not yours, if you had replied, "I thank you for the interview," then continued to stand, trust, and believe God, you would have had the right attitude. If you had been offered the position, you would have been happy; and if you had not been offered the position, you still would have been content. When the manager said to you that he had chosen another person for the position, you would continue to do all the things that you were doing before the manager's report. You wouldn't stop because you were not looking to the manager; you were looking to God to meet your need for a better position.

You continue to expect to be promoted, whether it is with the same company or another company with a better salary and benefits, but you put your trust in God and not in man!

Perhaps the person to whom the position had been offered may call and cancel because they were offered alternative employment, a position they preferred, or they just did not show up to work. The manager must choose you because you put your trust in God!

> Trust in the Lord with all your heart
> and lean not on your own understand-
> ing; In all your ways acknowledge Him,
> and He shall direct [you] your paths.
> (Proverbs 3:5)

My husband and I made the mistake of moving into a very bad apartment. We could not stay there and decided to move. After reaching an agreement with the property owner, we had sixty days to find a new home.

I believed God for an apartment with two bedrooms and two baths. We searched and found one that I liked tremendously. We filled out the forms, met all the requirements, and were approved. My husband and I did a high five; the deal was done at the end of December, and we looked forward to move on February 1st. We were told to expect a call telling us when to come and pay the first and last month's rent and get our keys.

In January, we received a call from the realty saying we had been denied and we were not getting the apartment!

Disappointed, we immediately started looking for another apartment and found one, but this apartment was smaller with two bedrooms and only one bathroom! Sadly, I didn't like it! I was not happy. I was fussing, and I had a negative attitude. I said to myself, "I wanted two bathrooms, not one!"

Time did not permit us to continue looking, and I heard the Holy Spirit say, "Be happy!"

I immediately changed my attitude and began to think about decorating the apartment, accepting the one bathroom. I stopped fussing with myself and was happy for the apartment.

And we continued to pack. Everything was set to go, and we were waiting for February to move into the two-bedroom, one-bathroom apartment, our second choice. Two weeks before we were to move, we received a call from the first apartment saying they had sent us an email—but we hadn't seen it! With all the preparation to move, we hadn't checked our emails! They wanted to know if we still wanted the apartment with two bedrooms and two bathrooms, as some things had changed and we could move in February 1st. I was so excited I could not contain myself. My husband asked me what I wanted to do—we would forfeit our deposit on the other apartment! I chose the apartment with two bedrooms and two bathrooms. We called the homeowner and told him we would not be renting with him. We moved into my heart-desired apartment with two bedrooms and two bathrooms. Glory to God!

In adversity, believe God. Keep on standing and trusting with a positive attitude because God is working it out for you. If things do not change immediately, be patient, because He wants to give you more, even abundantly more, than what you ask Him for or think you can have. Due Season doesn't have to be a long wait when your priorities are with God.

When you want something enough not to want it, you are now in faith, and peace will follow. Let us surrender all to Him, Jesus, our Blessed Savior. Let's surrender all to God. You don't know the plans God has for you. God has plans to prosper you, and you do not know how God is working out the plans. Everyone was born with a gift; you may have discovered that gift and know the purpose for it, but you don't know the plans. God has the plans and He knows how you are going to use the gift. When you seek Him, you will find Him when you seek Him with all your heart.

There is a difference between God's gift and talent. God has given the gifts (Ephesians 4:8). Talents are natural abilities, but you must practice to become proficient. But God's gift is already complete without practice, because a gift does not come from the natural world but the spiritual. There are gifted people, those who have received God's gifts—no doubt you can name some, and know some.

God gave the gift; you were born with the gift, and God knows the plans He has for your life. If you knew the plans and the gift together, you wouldn't need God. But to fulfill your purpose, God's purpose for you, here on earth, you need God that you may know your purpose, and his help to fulfill it. And God needs you to make his gift and his plan manifest, here on earth.

God may speak to people about you to answer your prayer request. God may speak to a person concerning what He wants them to do for you without your knowledge of what He is doing, but He will reveal to that person who it is and whom He wants to bless. God will speak to somebody about you, then He connects you together with that person to fulfill your prayer request, and distance does not limit God from connecting you to the answer. You don't know who God will choose to bless you. He may also speak to you about someone else who is standing in faith and belief. He chooses you to meet that person's needs. By meeting the needs of that person, your needs are also met. 2 Corinthians 9:8, "And God is able to bless you abundantly [*every favor and earthly blessing*] so that in all things at all times, having all that you need you will abound in every good work."

SEEDTIME AND HARVEST

There is a threefold usage of the word *seed* in scripture.

1. Agricultural seed: Christ's parable of the farmer.

    "The farmer held his seed in his upturned garment, casting it out as he walked. Grain was sown in the early winter, after the first rains" (The New Compact Bible Dictionary). "Listen! A farmer went out to plant some seed (see Mark 4:3–8).

2. Physiological seeds: of carnal generation and those of spiritual regeneration, the Bible speaks of incorruptible seed (see 1 Peter 1:23).

3. Figurative seeds are descendants, genealogy, ancestry, or a class of people (Genesis 12:7, 13:16; Ezra 2:59; Nehemiah 7:61).

The seed is the Word of God planted, and when it's watered with God's Word, which you speak, it brings forth a harvest of fruit after the kinds of words (seed) planted. In Luke 8:12, "Those by the wayside are they that hear; then comes the devil and takes away the word out of their hearts, lest they should believe and be saved." Also in Matthew 13:19, "When anyone hears the word of the kingdom, and does not understand it, then the wicked one comes and snatches away *the word* that was sown in his heart." According to your faith, whether little faith, great faith, or dead faith, **and even if watered, the seed will bring forth a little harvest, a great harvest, or a dead HARVEST.**

The seed planted will not produce a harvest if it's not watered with the word of God. James 2:17 says, "Even so faith, if it hath not works, is dead being alone." And Jesus says of the Roman centurion, "I have not found so great faith, no not in Israel" (Matthew 8:10). God takes care of the birds of the air. Do not worry about your life.

When you give money as a seed, you put a claim on your giving when you say, "I believe I received." You water the seed as you claim what you need. Do not leave your seed abandoned waiting to be claimed. When you say "I believe I have received," you are claiming your harvest; you are watering the seed. You plant it with your word for what you desire, and you water it with the Word. Claim the harvest for past seed sown. Say, "I received my harvest for my past seed sown."

Water every abandoned seed and call it in; claim it now. As a watering process, you keep the seed watered by speaking the Word of God pertaining to the seed. There is a growth process in the spiritual realm, just as there is in the natural. When a seed is planted in the natural soil, the bud doesn't come up the next day. Opposition may come to stop you from speaking what you believe and to stop your faith, but it will not succeed. You will not be denied.

Be confident in the word of God, not in yourself. Scripture says, "This is confidence we have in approaching God, that if we ask anything according to His will, He hears us. And if we know that He hears us, whatever we ask, we know that we have what we asked of him" (1 John 5:14–15).

Claim your harvest for the seed that you have planted, and claim the promises of God's Word. When you claim it, you are adding work to your faith. Faith and work brings in the harvest, so expect to receive your financial harvest; speak out your faith. Say, "I am financially secure now with all my financial needs met and all my debts are paid off." Say, "I have an abundant supply of money in my checking and savings account to meet my every need and to give to charitable causes." Jesus said to the blind man in Matthew 9:29, "According to your faith be it unto you." And in Mark 6:5–6, "And He could there do no mighty work, [except that He laid His hands upon a few sick people and healed them].

...And [yet] He marveled because of their unbelief." Your every thought and every word are seeds that will produce after its kind. The Word of God is a seed, and it brings forth after its kind. There are spiritual seeds and natural seeds, and both seeds need water to bring forth a harvest. The Word of God is also the water. Harvest depends on watering the soil in which the seed is planted that will cause the seed to grow and produce a harvest after its kind. Without water, the seed would wither, dry up, and die.

Different seeds are watered differently. When the seed is watered with the Word of God, it brings forth a harvest after its kind. You plant the seed by speaking the Word according to your needs, and you water it by speaking as if you have already received it. Positive words spoken will bring positive results, and negative words will bring negative results.

When words of doubt are spoken, they will produce dead results. Doubt is having two opinions. Do not think that you will receive when you doubt. Doubt is the enemy to the word of God; it stops God's word spoken in your heart. When doubt comes, it opposes faith. It is a spirit of lies, and it comes to kill, steal, and destroy the Word of God spoken and the seed planted. Jesus says, "The thief [Satan] comes to steal, and to kill and to destroy. I have come that they may have life, and that they might have it more abundantly" (John 10:10).

But when doubt comes to your mind, it is a sure sign that what you believe is true! Doubt comes to confirm what you believe, but if you do not resist doubt, it will steal what you believe. When doubt comes, know that you're winning. If you were losing, doubt would not have anything to oppose. Let doubt confirm that you are winning, that you have received what you believe. Do not fear doubt; doubt your doubt, and say, "I doubt that. Get out of my mind in the name of Jesus Christ." Speak to doubt. Don't think it; say it! Because doubt cannot hear your thoughts. Your spoken words of God are powerful, and doubt cannot answer you back.

When you think it, you have put yourself in the doubt arena, and the fight is unequal because the battle is in the mind, and you will lose every time. Fight the good fight of faith; it's a good fight because Jesus has already won the battle. The battle is not yours but the Lord's. Stand still and see the victory, and when you have done all that, you know what to do—stand. When you fight having armed yourself with the spoken word of God, which is the sword of the Spirit, and not with your mind, you are fighting on God's level and not the devil's.

Fear and doubt come to attack your belief of God's word, and wherever there is doubt, there is also fear. Whether you speak positive or negative words, watering the seed with those words will produce a harvest—one to life and the other to death. "Death and life are in the power of the tongue and those who love it shall eat its fruit" (Proverbs 18:21). The harvest depends on the water; the spoken word of God is the water that will produce fruit in your life. God is not holding back the harvest of the seed planted in the good ground of your heart. The seed that is planted in good soil and watered with the word of God will produce after its own kind. *Jesus was a seed planted on earth to bring forth a harvest of souls that no one can number to spend eternity with him forever.* In Genesis 8:22 it says, "As long as the earth remains, there will be planting and harvest, cold, and heat, summer and winter, day and night." The seed is the word of God. It is a spiritual seed; it produces life as the natural seeds produce life, and they both give food for life. A seed produces fruit, and the fruit comes in different seasons and for different reasons. Mind seeds are thought seeds and nature's seeds are for the many kinds of vegetables and fruit. All seeds have a purpose. 2 Corinthians 9:10, "Now He that supplies seed to the one sowing and bread for food will supply and multiply your seed for sowing, and increase the harvest [becoming] of your righteousness."

Many things in life begin with a seed, either a word seed or a thought seed. Every thought and every word spoken is a prayer seed; thoughts are unspoken words and are seeds planted in the mind, and seeds need regular watering daily or weekly. Whenever you have a need, you plant a seed with the word of God by speaking it, and then you water the seed by speaking God's word over it to bring results. When you are thinking on something, you're meditating on a seed thought. It's not the seed that brings the harvest but the ground in which the seed is planted. The heart is the ground where seeds are planted, and well-tended ground with good soil will bring forth an abundant harvest. Every seed will bring forth a harvest after its kind. Faith is to believe, and doubt, fear, and worry are three enemies of faith that will steal your harvest.

Jesus said to the leader of the synagogue, "Be not afraid, and only believe" (Mark 5:36).

Doubt eats away at faith and at truth and at belief constantly day and night, as waves from a storm at sea undermine and collapse an embankment. Doubt is having two opinions, a double mind where you go back and forth. At one moment, you're sure about a thing, and the next moment, you change your mind about it. James 1:7-8, "[F]or the doubter, being double-minded and unstable in all his ways, must not expect to receive anything from the Lord."

Fear is the absence of the truth, and when the truth comes in, fear disappears. With God's help I learned this and overcame a fear I had of driving on highways—I always drove on back roads. I lived in Boston, Massachusetts, and had joined a church an hour's drive distance by highway. Each time I drove to church an overwhelming fear would attack me. One day, I prayed and asked God to help me to overcome this fear, and this is how He answered my prayer.

I and a friend, Andrea, had been listening to a television ministry, The Word of Faith, founded on Mark 11:23-24, "[W]hoever says to this mountain, be lifted up and thrown into the sea, and does not waver in his heart but believes that what he says happens, so it will be for him. For this reason I say to you, everything which you pray and ask, believe that you receive it, and it will be so for you." They were having a two-week revival in Winter Haven, Florida and we decided to go. We planned to fly, but at the last moment my friend suggested we drive, 1,350 miles! At that point, I knew that God was about to answer my prayer. I was hesitant to travel on the highway, and I was about to face my fear; but suddenly a peace came over me, and I agreed for us to drive.

We left early in the morning at four o'clock before the morning-commute highway traffic and took turns driving. Every four hours we would exchange. Andrea was an experienced highway driver. We stopped at a shopping mall parking lot that night and rested for an hour and then continued to Florida. We stayed in Florida for one week attending the camp meeting and had breakfast, lunch, and dinner in an "all you can eat" diner, and our money was getting low! On the last day, we went to a restaurant where we were seated and then waited for about an hour before the waitress came to take our order. As a result, we asked to see the manager. He apologized and said the restaurant was terribly busy that day and for us to order whatever we wanted from the menu, free of charge. Coming back to Massachusetts, we stopped only to use the restroom. While I drove, Andrea even slept in the back seat! I was more comfortable driving back to Massachusetts, and I was no longer afraid of highway driving. Pray unceasingly. Every thought is a prayer, and every word is a prayer. The word of God says in Philippians 4:13, "I can do all things through Christ who strengthens me." God gave me the ability to travel from Boston, Massachusetts to Winter Haven, Florida, and I overcame the fear of highway driving.

YOUR LIFE PURPOSE

When you wait on God for your needs to be met, believe that what you are praying for has already been answered.

"I will answer them before they even call to me. While they are still talking about their needs, I will go ahead and answer their prayers" (Isaiah 65:24).

> Therefore I say to you, whatever things you ask when you pray, believe that you receive them, and you will have them. And whenever you stand praying, and if you have anything against anyone, forgive him that your Father in heaven may also forgive you your trespasses. But if you do not forgive, neither will your Father in heaven forgive your trespasses. (Mark 11:24–26)

The hindrance to prayer is unforgiveness. God always answers prayer. Whatever you ask when you pray, believe that you have received and so it shall be for you. It is not that God does not answer prayer, but maybe God's instruction is not followed. If you believe you shall receive what you prayed for and you wait for it, then you shall have, *"whatever you prayed for"* (Mark 11:24).

God works to accomplish and answer your prayer. But the answer to your prayer may be connected to others. You may be believing for a house, a job, or money to attend college. Many may have asked Him for the same things, and He is working in their lives also for them to receive. God answers before you ask, His answer immediate. Yet if it seem to you delayed, that is His angels making His word real for you.

God always answers. There are times we ask God to meet a need, but we are not prepared to receive the answer. Asking, hoping, expecting, having faith, loving: these are the assurance of your prayers, that what is not yet will be. Nor can these work apart; they need each other and work together. Everything you receive comes through love. Everything has a purpose; everyone has a purpose; you are here on earth for a purpose.

The earth was created for a purpose, and God made everything for a purpose. The light and the darkness were made for a purpose. The light was made to brighten the day, which is called the sun, and the darkness was made for rest and renewal for your body, which is called the night (see Genesis 1:1–5).

God has a purpose for everything that He has made, trees, birds, animals, earth, mankind. And He supplies the provision to fulfill that purpose. You came into the world with a purpose, and God has a plan for your life. He has the plan, and when you discover the purpose and desire of your heart and ask according to his will, He hears you. He did not bring you into the world without providing what you would need to fulfill that purpose.

Life is a gift from God but what you do with it is your choice. You can grow in God, finding and passionately fulfilling the promise that is your purpose, or you can abuse your gift.

Where God guides, He provides. He will provide for you and make a way for you to use the gift. God didn't give you the gift without His supervision. He knows the plans that He has for you to use the gift, and when you seek Him with all your heart, you will find Him and will know the plan. "To everything there is a season, and a time for every purpose under heaven" (Ecclesiastes 3:1).

The time for you to fulfill His plan for you, is appointed by Him. If you go ahead of Him before the appointed time, do not expect God to be waiting there for you! God's time is the right time, and when the time is right, nothing can stop you. Time itself is neutral and even-handed, judges no one, but does not wait. But the devil can cause you to waste it, and the gift in each moment wasted being a gift to the devil that you cannot get back!

And it is not your decision how it will come about or when, for that is God's plan, and if you go ahead of Him you will be on your own. His provision for you won't be there waiting for you! Wait for the appointed time, and everything you need will be waiting for you. Don't be like those in Matthew 7:21–23.

Jesus said to them, "Not everyone that says to me 'Lord, Lord' shall enter the kingdom of heaven but he that does the will of my Father which is in heaven. Many will say to me in that day, 'Lord, Lord, have we not prophesied in your name, and cast out devils in your name, have done many wonderful works? And then I will declare to them, 'I never knew you;' [*I did not send you*] depart from me you who practice iniquity."

Wait on the appointed time that God has for you. For as long as you are living, the time you have is yours as if a free gift of money to spend as you like. But in each moment is also God's gift for you, that only you, in yielding to sin and the devil, can steal from yourself. Therefore pray to realize God's gift in each moment, at the same time asking for guidance in your prayer. Do this and each moment will give you a richness, wealth, and prosperity of spirit. As the Scripture states,

Jesus became poor so that you might be made rich. (2 Corinthians 8:9)

The rich and the poor meet together; the Lord is the maker of them all. (Proverbs 22:2)

When you look at your neighbor's grass and it seems greener than yours, it is because your neighbors are using their time wisely by watering their grass, and they believe to fulfill their purpose. Likewise, you have received a gift, which is an exceeding abundant measure of time for you to use in your lifetime.

While you are looking at your neighbor's grass, you are neglecting yours. Use your time well and wisely and that use will guide you to God's purpose for you, whether directly or indirectly. Even if oppressed, God brings victory out of our difficulties, God will turn your trouble around and therefore do not let people, friends, families, strangers, or negative prophecy determine your life or your future.

When a child I was told I would not amount to anything in life! The one who should have given me guidance and love instead cursed my future, and for a long time I believed it and my life was very difficult. I didn't think that I would make it, but in time I saw that God loves me with an everlasting love. Jeremiah 31:3 says, "I have loved you with an everlasting love; therefore, with loving kindness have I drawn thee." God had a plan for my life that was good and gave me a hope and a future. I held onto that; I didn't let it go and I made it through. Find your purpose in your story.

What is your story? All life stories have a purpose. Your purpose in life is your story to bring God's glory and to help others. Everybody has a life story; you don't have to look for the story. Your life is the story that gives God the glory. Everyone has a different story; a story might be related but different from another person's story. Siblings each have a different story, and twins who are so closely related together in feelings and likeness have a different story. Find your story. God uses your difficulty—the abuse—to give you victory and bring freedom into your life. You don't know what God will use from your abuse. God shapes our experiences; the adverse experience was an asset, not a liability, the difficulty, and hardship you went through that almost killed you but didn't. Use the pain, the disappointment, the hurt, the loneliness, the rejection, the poverty; and tell others how you made it through and how you are still standing. You have graduated from life oppositions, and there are others that are just beginning life or going through what you went through; you have life ammunition to help them because of what you went through.

Maybe there was no one to mentor or encourage you and tell you that you can make it, but the voice within you kept speaking to you when you felt like you couldn't go on any longer. The voice that kept saying you can make it, keep on pushing, keep on believing, keep on standing, don't fall, there is something better on the other side. It didn't seem like God was with you because of the difficulties that you have gone through, but remember, "'For I know the plans I have for you,' declares the Lord, 'plans to prosper you and not to harm you, plans to give you hope and a future'" (Jeremiah 29:11).

The dreams and desires that you had in your heart that you didn't think you would ever accomplish but you did. Let hope rise in you to guide you through. Many have lived through difficult times with long years of wondering if things will ever get better, but time is on your side. As long as you have breath and as long as you have life and determination, you will make it through. This is a song by Andrea Crouch that has helped me to make it through. "Through it all, through it all, I've learned to trust in Jesus, I've learned to trust in God. Through it all, through it all, I've learned to depend on His Word." The difficulty, the hard life, and the pain don't last forever! Never give up! Some are depending on you. And many waiting for your help. You may not know who they are, but when they read your life story or hear how you made it through, they will be encouraged and motivated to go on living. Knowing you have made it through, they also can make it through.

You receive by faith, but what is faith? "It is the confident assurance that something you want is going to happen. It is the certainty of what we hope for is waiting for us, even though we cannot see it up ahead" (Hebrews 11:1). Give your dreams and desires life; begin to see yourself out of the situation that you're in. The dream in your heart doesn't have to wait to be recognized by others; you are the first to recognize it and see yourself in it. If you need to complete your education, see yourself standing on the platform wearing your cap and gown and all the people, including your family and friends waving at you, clapping and shouting praises. See the end results.

God makes known the end from the beginning, and He speaks the end results (see Isaiah 46:10).

Remember that God has a hope and a future for you; see your future. There are those who have different kinds of dreams and desires. It doesn't matter what your dream and desires are. See the end results from the beginning, and see yourself as an accomplished person. God would not have given you the gift if He didn't have a purpose for you to use the gift. *Satan cannot read your mind, so he doesn't know God's plan for you.* The Word of God says in James 4:7, "Submit yourselves therefore to God. Resist the devil, and he will flee from you." *Submit to God and His Word of truth.*

HAVING DONE ALL STAND

Having done all, stand, and stand on what you believe God for. Stand on God's word, and rightly divide the Word. If the Word can be rightly divided, it also can be wrongly divided. The Holy Spirit helps us to rightly divide the Word. Scripture states, **"But the anointing which you have received from Him abides [lives] in you, and you don't need that anyone teach you; but as the same anointing teaches you concerning all things, and is true, and is not a lie, and just as it has taught you, you will abide in Him"** (1 John 2:27).

God said you do not need anyone to teach you, but by His Spirit, He teaches you through the anointing how to rightly divide His word. Jesus gave to the church "apostles, prophets, evangelists, pastors, and shepherds to equip the saints for the work of the ministry,... until we all come into the unity of the faith and a fuller knowledge of the Son of God unto a perfect (*mature*) person, unto the measure of the stature of the fullness of Christ" (Ephesians 4:11–13).

As well as with the Word of God and the Holy Spirit, pastors, and teachers are there to equip you to both know God and to know and accomplish His work in you. Thus not to be like children blown about by every wind of new teaching and to receive God's word so as to rightly divide the word of truth. Second Timothy 2:15, "Study to show thyself approved unto God a workman that need not to be ashamed, rightly dividing the word of truth."

God speaks to you through His Word which is hidden in your hearts so that you don't sin against Him. As He teaches you, remain in fellowship with Christ, living as a child of God. Let the anointing that you have received from Him abide in you, and it will bring revelation of His word to you, and the light of His word will shine so brightly that you will see it as never before. As His word is revealed in all things, its truth will teach you to abide in Him, as it says in John 15:26, "But when the comforter is come, whom I will send unto you from the father, even the Spirit of truth, which proceeds from the father, He shall testify of me."

The Comforter, the Holy Spirit, sent in Jesus's name, shall remind you of God's word in you. And having that and the Holy Spirit in you, you shall not need anyone to further teach you what is true. For the Spirit teaches you everything you need to know, and as He has taught you, "abide in Him." (1 John 2:27)

Have faith in God! In Hebrews 11:6, we read, "But without faith it is impossible to please Him, for He who comes to God, must believe that He is, and that He is a rewarder of those who diligently seek Him." And He has already given you the measure of that faith you need to believe (see Romans 12:3). Jesus couldn't do any mighty miracles in His own country because they didn't believe; He only healed a few sick people. "And because of their unbelief, he couldn't do any miracles among them unless to place his hand on a few sick people" (Mark 6:5). Faith is the confidence of what we hoped for will actually happen; it gives us assurance about things we cannot see. Hope is expectancy that faith needs, for without hope, faith can't work. Faith, hope, and love—without love, faith cannot work. Faith and love go together, and one cannot work without the other. "Faith without works is dead" (James 2:26).

Inactive faith without works is dead; they both need each other to produce and bring forth results, the desired results. You believed that you received it without the evidence of seeing it. In the presence of fear and doubt, keep on speaking what you believe until it is manifested. Faith cannot be explained; it's the confidence of what we hoped for will actually happen. Faith believes and speaks the word of God. **Faith calls those things which do not exist as though they did.**

Faith is the confidence of the expected results of what you hoped for. There are those who hope to be married, to have a house, to be healed, go to college, have a job, and to prosper; it is God's will that you prosper in spirit, soul, and body and be in health even as your soul prospers (3 John 1:2).

Hope is the expectancy of what you desire you will receive, and faith speaks into manifestation the things that are not seen: "Let the weak say I am strong" (Joel 3:10). *Speak it into existence. Let the sick say I am healed, let the poor say I am rich.* The scripture says in Proverbs 23:7, "For as he thinks in his heart, so is he." To think in your heart is to believe. When you delight in the Lord, He shall give you desires of your heart. "Now this is the confidence that we have in Him, that if we ask anything according to His will, He hears us. And if we know that He hears us, whatever we ask, we know that we have the petitions that we have asked of Him" (1 John 5:14, 15).

And Isaiah 65:24, "Before we ask, God hears us, and while we are praying, He answers."

Enemies of faith are fear and worry. Faith is the opposite of fear; faith believes; it's the confident assurance that something we want is going to happen. Fear also believes, that something we don't want is going to happen. Faith is to believe the truth, and fear is to believe a lie. Worry is thinking that what you don't want is going to happen; it's meditating on the negative results of something. It drains your energy and strength. Worrying brings fear and torment.

Therefore I tell you, do not worry about your life, what you will eat or drink; or about your body, what you will wear. Is not life more than food and the body more than clothes? Look at the birds of the air; they do not sow or reap or store away in barns, and yet your heavenly Father feeds them. Are you not much more valuable than they? Can anyone of you by worrying add a single hour to your life?

And why do you worry about clothes? See how the flowers of the field grow. They do not labor or spin. Yet I tell you that not even Solomon in all his splendor was dressed like one of these. If that is how God clothes the grass of the field, which is here today and tomorrow is thrown into the fire, will He not much more clothe you; you of little faith? So do not worry, saying, "What shall we eat?" or "What shall we drink?" Or "What shall we wear?" For the pagans run after all these things, and your heavenly Father knows that you need them. But seek first His kingdom and His righteousness, [*His way of doing things*] and all these things will be given to you as well. Therefore do not worry about tomorrow, for tomorrow [*tomorrow becomes today*] will worry about itself. Each day has enough trouble of its own. (Matthew 6:25–34)

God wants you to put Him in remembrance of what He has spoken in His Word. He listens for your voice of His word to do it. Meditate on the scriptures pertaining to what you believed you received.

Put me in remembrance; Let us plead together; declare thou that thou (you) may be justified. (Isaiah 43:26)

SPIRITUAL STORM RATED

When the storm comes, say, "This too shall pass." Double up in reading God's Word and prayer, and if you have received your spiritual language, pray in that language. In Jude 1:20, it says, "But you, beloved, building yourselves up on your most holy faith, praying in the Holy Spirit, keep yourselves in the love of God." Spend time praising and worshipping God. In Psalms 100, we read, "Come into God's presence with singing, into His gates with thanksgiving and into His courts with praise." Determine that the storm season will be short. Also be silent in the storm, not quiet but silence!

In the storm, I used my carnal words to defend myself. I was not aware that the battle I was in was not a carnal battle but a spiritual battle! Now I have learned how to prepare for it and how to have victory in the storm. Every marital storm is a spiritual battle won only with spiritual weapons (see 2 Corinthians 10:3, 4). Natural weapons are no match for the storm, for it is unseen like the wind, and before you know it, you are blown about like the dry leaves that fall from the trees.

All storms are fought from the heavenly realm with spiritual weapons. You cannot see the wind, and you cannot see the storm before it comes; but it destroys whatever is in its path like a tornado, and sometimes a marital storm will seem like a tornado.

Marital storms are not with flesh and blood but with unseen wicked spirits like the unseen wind. The wind comes before the storm. When you feel the wind and see the leaves blowing, you cannot see what is causing it, but you can see the effect and damage the wind may make. Just like a storm in your marriage, you cannot see the wind, but you experience the influence and the effect of its destruction in your marriage.

The unseen spirits are like the wind; the effect can be the arguments, harsh words, the separation, the divorce. These are all the effects of the storm. Some storms pass, but others are very destructive like a tornado destroying everything in its path. Don't wait for the storm to surprise you by its suddenness. Surprise it when it comes; be ready with your armor on (Ephesians 6:11–18) to endure its force and prevail. Do not let the storm destroy your marriage. There are natural and spiritual storms that bring destruction, and they can be fought with the same weapons. The weapon, the sword of the Spirit (the Word of God) can calm the weather and the storms of the sea. Jesus did it in Luke 8:23–24. He used the weapon, the word of God. He spoke the word and rebuked the waves of the storm and it ceased. The word of God can conquer all storms. The spoken word of God can calm the storms (arguments) with the word of love. God tells us to walk in love as Christ also has loved us (Ephesians 5:2).

As a child of God no storm can prevail over you. You are safe in the protection of God's word. And you need only be ready when it comes, whether against your marriage, your health, your children, or anything else. Put on your armor, and use God's power in you. In enduring, surviving, prevailing over the storm you are more than a conqueror through Christ Jesus (Romans 8:37), to calm every storm that comes to you and win every battle that comes against you.

In a natural storm, you don't wait for the storm to appear before you buy food and water to stock up or board up your windows and have batteries and a flashlight. There are those who have a storm cellar stocked with whatever is needed to last out the storm! They are not waiting for the last moment; they are already prepared.

If the response to the natural storm's warning can be so effective for those who obey it, how much more should the spiritual storm warning be obeyed? God always warns us before a storm comes. You listen to the natural storm warning; you prepare for it; and it didn't destroy you. Heed His warning and shall you not be even safer in any spiritual storm? Yet many of God's people don't prepare for those storms that come into their lives.

Jesus says in John 16:33 that in this world, you will have trouble (*storms*), but to be encouraged because He has already overcome them. And He has given to you the instructions you need in *His Word,* just as does civil authority for a natural storm. Jesus has overcome them and has given you His word to stand against the storms when they come. Put His word into effect so then you can be encouraged because you were warned and prepared yourself to stand in the storm. And having this, you can then stand confidently.

A spiritual storm is different from natural storms, and the things needed to prepare for the storm are different. In the spiritual storm, you need the word of God to light your path. In Psalms 119:105 says, "Your word is a lamp to guide my feet and a light for my path."

In the natural storm, you stock up on natural food. In the spiritual storm, you need the word of God; it's your spiritual food and water, so you stock up on the word before the storm comes. Jesus is the bread of life, and as you read His Word, you will never thirst or be hungry (John 6:35). You can't use natural resources to fight a spiritual storm, but you can use spiritual resources to fight a natural storm, for example, the storm of sickness. The scripture says in 1 Peter 2:24, "He [Jesus] himself bore our sins in His body on the cross so that we might die to sins and live for righteousness, by his wounds you have been healed."

If your storm is lack, "The Lord is my shepherd; I have all that I need" (Psalms 23:1). A natural storm is connected to the weather, in the natural realm, but a spiritual storm is connected to the unseen realm, and it needs spiritual preparation to pass the storm. You will be able to stand against every storm that comes against you when your house is built on the rock. Matthew 7:24 says it this way: "Anyone who listens to my teaching and follows it is wise, like a person who builds a house on solid rock." The word of God never changes. The storm must pass. The storm doesn't come to stay, and when you are prepared, there might be a small amount of damage or no damage at all, and you will be standing. The scripture says, "Having done all, stand" (see Ephesians 6:13). There are those who couldn't stand, and their house was washed away by the flood. They didn't obey the warning before the storm came, so there wasn't the time to prepare; it was too late, and God was blamed for their lack of preparation.

You hear people of God say, when they pray, God doesn't always say yes or answer their prayers. For example, "He didn't answer when I prayed and asked Him to protect my marriage." Or, "When the doctor said I had cancer, I prayed and fasted and asked God to heal me, and He didn't! Now the doctor says the cancer is incurable. Where is God? He promised that if I asked for anything according to His will, He hears me." As in 1 John 5:14, if this cancer is not according to His will, why doesn't He heal me? It's not in the middle of a storm we remind God of His promises; it's before the storm comes! God says before you call (*prayed*), He answered; and while you're speaking, He hears you (see Isaiah 65:24). It's when you are cancer-free and standing on His word, reading His promises and reminding Him of what He promised in His Word; and when the storm comes, you are under the shelter of His word. You can stand, and instead of blaming God, you will be praising Him for His goodness and His mercy and His answer to your prayers.

The house built on the sand (Matthew 7:26–27) illustrates the person who uses his own natural resources to build his house. He chooses his own lifestyle, seeking things of this world apart from God and making his own life decisions. Many of God's people are building their house (life) on the sand without God and not on the rock, Christ Jesus. When the rain descends and the flood comes and the wind blows and beats upon that house, it will fall! When the storms of life come, sickness, divorce, eviction (*and storms will come*), you will not be able to stand.

In a financial storm, say, "I do not believe what I see or hear. In the absence of finances, I will trust God, and in the presence of finances, I will trust God. I am not willing to give place to fear, doubt, or worry in my thoughts. What God has for me is for me, and no one can have what is mine."

When I receive the manifestation of what I believe God for, I will continue to confess, "I believe, that I receive." I will keep my faith active. I am trusting in God to meet my need. I don't give my faith a break; faith works. God has a plan for my life, and He knows the path and the way. Acknowledge Him in all your ways, and He will guide you. You might say, "There are those who are unbelievers, and they don't crumble when the storm comes." It's only because of the mercy of God they are helped, but you have the promises of God—the word of God and His mercy. God has given the believers over 3000 promises in His Word to stand against the storm, which the unbelievers don't have access to, and it's because they can't come boldly to the throne of God's grace (see Hebrews 4:16). The ungodly are not so but are like the chaff, which the wind drives away. Therefore, the ungodly shall not stand in the judgment of sinners in the congregation of the righteous. For the lord knows the way of the righteous, but the way of the ungodly shall perish (Psalms 1:4–6). Trust God when things are rough, and trust Him when things are smooth. Be not afraid of adversity. When pressure comes, open your mouth and speak the word of God. Cast all your care upon Him, for He cares for you. "Fear not, doubt not, and worry not." Do not look at the storm of adversity; trust God and have no fear. Have a positive attitude, and don't give place to fear, doubt, or worry.

STORM SCRIPTURES

(Say or pray the Scriptures)

Isaiah 25:4
For thou has been a strength to the poor,
strength to the needy in His distress, a refuge
from the storm, a shade from the heat;
Lord you have been my strength in time of need
and in distress refuge from the storm and a
shadow from the heat.

Psalms 2:12
"Blessed are those who put their trust in Him."
I am blessed because I put my trust in God.

Psalms 3:3
"But You, Oh Lord, are a shield for me. My glory
and the one who lifts up my head."
You, Lord are a shield around me my glory
the one who lifts my head high. The one who
holds my head high.

Psalms 3:6
"I will not be afraid of ten thousands of people who have
set themselves against me all around."
I will not be afraid though ten *thousands* of people have
set themselves against me.

Psalms 4:3
"But know that the Lord has set apart for Himself him
who is godly; the Lord will hear when I call to Him."
I know that the Lord has set me
apart for Himself. The Lord
will hear me when I call [pray] to Him.

Psalms 5:3
"My voice you shall hear in the morning, O Lord;
in the morning I will direct it to you, and I will look up."

Psalms 5:12
"For you, O Lord, will bless the righteous, with favor
You will surround him as with a shield."
The Lord will bless I the righteous with favor
and surround me with favor as with a shield.

Psalms 6:9
The Lord has heard my supplication; the Lord
will receive my prayer.

Psalms 23:6
Surely goodness and mercy shall follow me
All the days of my life; and I will dwell in the
house of the Lord forever.

Psalms 25:5
Lead me to your truth and teach me; for you
are the God of my salvation; and on you
do I will wait all the day.

Psalms 27:14
Wait on the Lord; Be of good courage,
And He shall strengthen your heart: wait, I say,
on the Lord!
I wait on the Lord and I am of good courage
and He strengthens my heart to wait.

Psalms 32:8
I will instruct you and teach you in the
way you should go; I will guide you with my eye.
Lord, instruct me and teach me in the way
In which I shall go, guide me with your eyes.

Psalms 91:10, 11
There shall no evil befall thee, neither
shall any plague, [sickness] come
nigh thy dwelling. For He shall give
His angels charge over
thee to keep thee in all thy ways.
There shall no evil come to me, neither will any

Plague comes to my home. God
shall give his angels charge
over me to keep me in all my ways.

Psalms 37:3–5
Trust in the Lord, and do good, dwell in the land,
And feed on His faithfulness.
Delight yourself also in the Lord, and He shall
give you the desires of your heart.
Commit your way to the Lord, trust also in him
and He shall bring it to pass.
I trust in the Lord and I do good and I live in the
land and I am fed. I delight myself in the Lord,
and He gives me the desires of my heart.
I commit my way unto the Lord and trust
Him and He will bring it to pass.

Psalms 34:7
The angel of the Lord encamps all around those who
fear [respect] Him, and He delivers them.
The angel of the Lord encamps around me; I respect
the Lord and He delivers me.

Proverbs 16:3
Commit your works to the Lord, and
your thoughts will be established.
I commit my work unto the Lord and my
thoughts are established

Psalms 34:4
I sought the Lord, and He heard me,
and delivered me from all my fears.

Psalms 46:1
God is our refuge and strength, a very
present help in trouble.
God is my refuge and my strength
a very present help when trouble comes.

Proverbs 18:10
The name of the Lord is a strong tower; the
righteous run to it and are safe.
The name of the Lord is a high tower, and I the righteous
runs into it and I am safe

SALVATION

If you believe in Jesus, you will not perish [*die*] but have eternal life. God sent His Son, Jesus, to pay the penalty for sin; He died on the cross, was buried, and God raised Him to life again. The scripture says in John 3:16–17, "For God so loved the world that He gives His one and only son, that whoever believe in him shall not perish, but have eternal life." For God didn't send His Son into the world to condemn the world but to save the world. *Through Adam's disobedience, which is eternal death,* many *were made sinners.* For as by one man's disobedience, many were made sinner; so by the obedience of one *(Jesus)* shall many be made righteous (Romans 5:19). Adam's sin brought punishment to all, but Jesus's obedience to the cross made mankind right with God.

To receive the gift of salvation, Romans 10:9 says, "If you declare (say) with your mouth Jesus is Lord, and believe in your heart God raised Him from the dead, you will be saved."

If you believed and prayed that prayer, you are now saved. When you're saved, your spirit is born again; you become a new creation (2 Corinthians 5:17). Therefore if any man (person) be in Christ, **he is a new creature: old**

things are passed away. Behold, all things are become new. You received a gift. "For it is by grace you have been saved through faith; and this is not from yourselves; it is the gift of God" (Ephesians 2:8).

Join a Christian faith-based Bible-believing church and attend classes for your spiritual growth and become part of a church family. Begin a habit of reading the Bible. Start reading from the Gospel of John, and grow in God's grace.

ABOUT THE AUTHOR

Minister Grace Neils Woodbridge attended Cambridge College in Cambridge, Massachusetts. She graduated Faith Fellowship Ministry Victory Bible School and also their School of Advanced Leadership Training. She is an ordained minister and member of the National Association Christian Ministers (NACM). She is a certified marriage and premarriage coach, as well as an evangelist and  teacher-preacher of the ministry of the Word of God via reconciliation, with an emphasis on salvation. Minister Grace believes that she has been anointed by God to bring good news (the Gospel) to the suffering and the afflicted. To comfort the broken heart, to announce freedom to the captives, and to tell people that the time of God's favor has come.

She is East Indian and African Caribbean, descendant of Benin, Africa. She resides in Tyngsborough, Massachusetts, with her husband. Her autobiography is titled *Grace from Joyce to Grace*.

CPSIA information can be obtained
at www.ICGtesting.com
Printed in the USA
LVHW032109260121
677513LV00002B/256